RUB SOME DIRT ON IT.

BY BOBBY BONNER

LIVING
FAITH
BOOKS

Copyright © 2022 by Bobby Bonner. All scripture quotations are taken from the King James Authorized Version.

First published in 2022 by Living Faith Books.

All rights reserved. This book or parts thereof may not be reproduced in any form, stored in any retrieval system, or transmitted in any form by any means—electronic, mechanical, photocopy, recording, or otherwise—without prior written permission of the publisher and/or author, except as provided by United States of America copyright law.

Living Faith Books
3953 Walnut St
Kansas City, MO 64111

Creative Director: Joel Springer
Chief Editor: Melissa Wharton
Cover Design: Brandon Briscoe
Formatting: Joel Springer
Page Editing: Becca Bagunu
ISBN: 978-1-950004-19-5
Printed in the United States of America

Contents

Foreword	7
Introduction	9
Chapter 1: Youth	11
Chapter 2: Adulthood and Salvation	17
Chapter 3: Seeking Truth	23
Chapter 4: I Got Traded	29
Chapter 5: Seeking God's Face	33
Chapter 6: Being Sent	39
Chapter 7: Zambia	45
Chapter 8: Missionary vs. Missionary	51
Chapter 9: Fear God, Not Man	59

Foreword

As I sat down and read Bobby Bonner's new work, I couldn't help but feel that I was actually in his presence as he shared much of his own personal life and thoughts. Intimate is a good word to describe this book. Bobby is very transparent, and that is always refreshing when reading someone's autobiography. There are no frills here!

Bobby has always been a fierce competitor, at least since a young age when his older family members got his attention and challenged him. His competitive spirit cannot be squelched, but it finds its way to the surface through genuine gratitude and humility before the Lord.

Bobby's journey and experiences reflect many a missionary's struggles, blessings, and frustrations. These people are select and unusual individuals. They are formed to carry out the most wonderful—yet difficult—of assignments. They must be tough and committed.

Bobby Bonner has been one of my heroes for as long as I can remember. A great preacher, teacher, missionary, and friend, Bobby has been a wonderful example to me, enriched my life, and given me courage to compete for the gospel.

Dr. George Grace
Pastor of First Bible Baptist Church

Introduction

What, another book? After writing a few stories about my life as a professional baseball player-turned-missionary to Africa in the book From the Diamond to the Bush, much has happened when it comes to what I have seen and learned from others. Our lives are like a book, read of all people as Paul describes it in 2 Corinthians 3:2 — "Ye are our epistle written in our hearts, known and read of all men."

My older brothers, Sid and KK, were great athletes and competitors who pushed me and drove me to be competitive in everything, even relationships. They would play catch with me and almost every time end up making me cry by inflicting some sort of pain. They would always tell me, "Stop crying, baby. Rub some dirt on it. Get back out there." I was being sharpened through competition. Some don't like confrontation or competition, but in my childhood, it was a daily routine and way of life that fashioned my worldview and thought processes.

Believers in Jesus Christ, however, are being fashioned by the Master. He takes us through trials and tribulations, molding us into the image of our Savior, with our flesh and the world's system fighting against us the whole way. Gang, we are in a war, a competition. Each born-again believer should know that there is victory awaiting us! There are two times to serve God: when you feel like it and when you don't. So rub some dirt on it and get back in the game! It ain't over!

My life has always been an open book. People have their opinions of the motives or the actuality of certain events, but only the Lord knows our hearts and the true motives behind why we do what we do. In any event, I will try to pen some things down that I have seen and learned over the years which could bring a smile to your face or a question to your mind, or maybe an occasion for us to step into a closer walk with the Lord. That is my prayer. I write not to condemn, but to contend. I write not to judge hearts, but to judge righteous judgment. I write not for my own glory, but that my God, the Lord Jesus Christ, would receive all the glory, for this is all because of Him, to Him, and through Him.

As you enter the pages and memories of my life, please know that I hold no grudges. I only tell the stories as I remember them and the lessons learned along the way. As you contemplate your own life and the lessons that you've learned, I hope that even among the trials and tribulations that you faced, you have come through and risen up to get back in the game. Jesus is worth it all!

Chapter One
Youth

As I begin to share memories from my teen years, I do so with fear and thankfulness. I fear because I do not want to glorify sin and rebellion. I fear because I do not want my children and grandchildren to experience the sin and heartache that I went through as a young man trying to find out who I was and what love was all about, how to make friends—and go through puberty in the midst of all that.

But I also share with thankfulness to the Lord for saving my soul. I am thankful for the blood of Jesus that has washed away my sin and the restoration and forgiveness it brings.

I grew up west of San Antonio, Texas, up in what is called the hill country. I grew up exploring the countryside and caves, swimming in rivers, riding horses, and playing out pretend epics with my cousins who were my best friends. We were always playing sports, competing with one another. I also had older brothers who were local sports heroes, and this created in me a spirit of competition.

Once, my brothers caught a nanny goat and held it up to all us boys and said that in order for us to get big and strong like them, we had to suck on its teats and drink some milk. Of course, the oldest cousin, Bronco, took hold and began to suck. Tom, Buster, and I took off and refused to do it. A few years ago, Bronco reminded me of that story. Of all the cousins, Bronco had grown up the shortest of the bunch. He laughed at the story and said, "Your brothers lied to me." Soon after, my family left the innocent ranch life and moved to the big Texan city of Corpus Christi. Going from a population of 350 to over 250,000 was a change.

We moved to Corpus Christi the summer before I entered seventh grade. One of my older brothers, KK, had a friend who was a little league coach and had asked him if I could be on the team. Even though my family lived in another area of town, my brother put down his address for me so I could play on his friend's team with his son. I began to play at what was called Padre Little League. My first friends were on that team. It was also how I entered the sports world. We had some great seasons there at Padre and almost went to the Little League World Series, but we lost the game that would have put us at Williamsport.

Like I said, my parents lived on the other side of town. When I started school, it was in a different district from all my little league friends. All the other boys at my school played with the Oso Pony Baseball League. On top of that, the kids around me were all into the beach, surf boards, longer hair, marijuana, rock music (it was the early 60s, after all), along with football, basketball, and track. And here I was, a redneck in boots and short hair—the odd man out.

So, I dove into all four sports that were offered at Cullen Junior High to make friends. At the end of each school year, awards were given out for several things. One was to the most athletic player in the school. I received this award each year I was there. Sports had become my outlet, my identity. And competition was in my DNA.

I made some friends who were all good players and accepted me into their "tribe." I played sports with these guys during the school year, played summer ball with and against them, went to the beach, fished, hung out, and went to movies (especially the drive in) with them. One thing of note is that they were all of different faiths. One was a Catholic, another a Baptist, and my best friend went to a Church of Christ. When I would stay with them from time to time, I would attend church with them. I was never really brought up in church, but I believed there was a God, though I did not know Him. I believed in heaven and hell; I was not a fool.

When I entered high school, I knew my grades would count for graduation, so I had to buckle down. I was a pretty good student, making all As and Bs without really trying. Football season started, and I was the starting quarterback. My girlfriend was the head cheerleader. Life was great. Then a huge linebacker came and hit me so hard all the tendons and muscles in my left knee were torn.

I had suffered an awful injury. While I was in the hospital coming out of surgery, the phone in my room rang. It was my girlfriend. She had called to break up with me. The next day, she began to go steady with the starting halfback, who was one of my four best friends. I was devastated. My rehab was long and grinding. Watching the games from the sidelines, being unable to compete, and seeing the accolades coming to all the other players brought heavy depression.

A few weeks after the surgery, my buddies asked one of their older brothers to take us to see a movie at the Viking Twin Drive-In theater. I was still on crutches at the time. While there, my buddies were giggling and headed off away from the car. I saw something in their hands along with some matches. I yelled for them to wait up, but they said, "You don't want to do this." I said, "Man, yes I do." So I smoked my first joint. I should have listened to them, but I felt I needed these guys. I was so depressed with the injury and the breakup, so I started smoking dope from that day, every day. For the next nine years, there was seldom a day that went by when I did not light one up. Marijuana was my friend. It helped me forget my problems, though they never seemed to go away. And once again, competition set in. Now I wanted to smoke more than anyone, outdrink anyone. I was so tall as a young man that I never needed a fake ID and got into lots of clubs before I was 18.

Before long, I hurt my knee again. Within a year, I was under the knife again. Once again, the drugs and alcohol seemed a relief. One night while driving around in the back of our friend's older brother's car, we had smoked about ten doobies, and, between the four of us, drunk a case of beer. We ran out of weed and booze, so we took a spray can of acrylic and sprayed it into a paper bag to huff.

The next morning when my mom came into my room, she screamed. There was blood all over my doorknob and door, my sheets. My face was covered in dried blood and my shirt was ripped, along with my trousers. She woke me up and demanded to know what happened. The only thing I could remember was that before the night's real festivities started, we were jumping on a trampoline. I told her I fell off. I could not remember what really happened. The next day, my friends were laughing and telling me what I had been doing. Apparently, I got up on a dumpster and began to dive into a parking lot full of gravel. After the fourth or fifth time, I had knocked myself out and blood flowed from my face, head, chest, and knees. They took me home and somehow got me inside without waking my parents. They threw me on the bed with all my clothes on. I could have died that night and woken up in hell. Boy, am I thankful that was not the case.

Towards the end of high school, I was living a double life. The life of a student athlete—obedient to some degree—and my other life of drugs, alcohol, and girls. No matter what I was involved with, it was about trying to be the best, whether it was working out, running, lifting weights, doing drugs, or drinking. I worked hard and I played harder. I remember my dad telling me once that he knew what I was up to and that if I was ever busted not to call him.

As I entered my junior year of high school, I had another operation on my other knee. I lied and told people it was a sports injury, but I had actually been in a motorcycle wreck. I was popping wheelies down the street while high as a kite, and the back wheel went up on a curb and I went flying. Once again, the drugs and alcohol continued. Then along came experimenting with LSD, mescaline, mushrooms—all kinds of illegal drugs, trying to escape my depression. It was the late 60s and early 70s now, and the time of peace, love, and the sexual revolution was in full swing. And of course I wanted in on all that too.

The summer after my junior year, a girl and I found ourselves caught up in the consequences of sin. She was pregnant and I was the father-to-be. I had gone away for the summer to live with my older brother and work near Houston. When I returned, my phone rang and I was told the news. We met and talked it over. We were both too young to marry. How would we raise this child? Even though we were not Christians, neither of us believed we should kill this unborn baby boy. After telling my parents and speaking with those involved, it was decided between us that we would give the baby up for adoption.

My senior year was not what I thought it would be. Instead of ruling the school, I was miserable. I felt even worse for my ex-girlfriend up until because of the gossip about and shame towards her from our school. Self-ishly, I almost transferred to another high school across town when my brother offered that to me. No girl wanted to date me, and I did not blame them. I was awful, using everyone in my path for self-gratification. I was so depressed I almost took my life one night, putting a shot gun in my mouth but too afraid to pull the trigger.

A while after, one of my friends asked me if we could go on a double date together. He had a crush on this girl named Becky Petty. She was a sophomore and I was a senior. Because no girls at school would date me, I was dating a girl who had already graduated, and we all went out. That night, Becky and I talked and talked, and a few days later I saw her at a party. I walked up to her and kissed her, and I knew she was the one for me. I felt I had found someone so real, so fulfilling, that I quit the hard stuff and just smoked some dope and drank.

I made it through my senior year and was chosen to participate in the very first Texas Highschool All-State baseball game to be played in the Astrodome in Houston. I was chosen nation-wide as the best shortstop coming out of high school, making All-American Honors. I was drafted by the Montreal Expos in the tenth round as a pitcher. They offered a pretty good signing bonus plus the college of my choice. My older brother met with me and talked me into going to college first; I'd be the first one in the family to do so. I was offered many scholarships to different schools, mainly as a pitcher because of my arm and accuracy. The coach from Texas A&M came and offered me a full ride to play shortstop. I chose to accept because I wanted to play every day, and this was my chance.

As I headed off to college, my heart was still in the Sparkling City by the Sea, so I would skip class on Fridays, drive to Corpus Christi, and spend the weekend with Becky. On Mondays I would drive back to A&M, of course skipping more classes.

My coach called me into his office one day and told me that my professors called him and told him I was flunking out of school because of my attendance. I told him I was in love and spending each moment I had with Becky Petty. He asked me if I wanted to marry her, and I said yes. What follows is an amazing story. Coach called Becky's father and asked him if I could drive down the next weekend to marry Becky so I could bring her back and get an apartment with married housing on campus. And he said YES. My life would forever change that day. I was 18 years old (Becky was 17), a freshman in college, not understanding life but knowing how to work hard and play hard.

The next four years at Aggieland—competing at the highest level when it came to collegiate sports—I began to make a name for myself. Scouts were at most of our games. We had some great talent in those days and won the Southwest Conference title for baseball in both '77 and '78, back-to-back championships. The competition during those years was crazy. I had to rub a lot of dirt on it. But now that I had a wife, a young child, and another on the way, the competition of my youth was now coming to an end. I had to think about what the future would be. I decided it would be professional baseball, as a player first and one day as a coach. My direction was set, and I was drafted in the third round by the Baltimore Orioles. I thought I was on my way.

Chapter Two
Adulthood and Salvation

Life changed drastically for me when I got married. I was just 18 years old, and a competition between my youth and the idea of becoming a man was taking place inside of me. I understood right from wrong and could tell from creation that there is a God. But I rebelled against that, rejecting God over and over, because I didn't think that God could love a person who was so full of himself, so full of pride, rebellion, and sin. Ultimately, I cared for no one but myself.

My inner turmoil over the next four years of college drove me to stay as busy as I could in as many areas as I could. I worked very hard on the field and I played just as hard off the field. Drinking, boozing, smoking dope, staying out all night at times, waking up somewhere in the athletic dorm or my car—one time in a ditch. I was on a fast-track to destruction.

At one point, Becky went to visit her parents for a few days, so I invited my buddies over for a party which lasted a couple of days. After drinking all day Saturday, I took a dozen downers, passed out, and woke up Tuesday morning in a bed full of nearly every bodily fluid. Becky was still out of town, and my friends just left me in that state and never checked on me. I could not believe I had once again survived my stupidity. The battle raged in my mind: could anyone really love the real me? I was once again living a double life. I stopped with the pills, but still smoked dope and drank every day, trying to drown out the battle in my mind.

On the diamond, I was working hard every day to fulfill my dreams of one day playing in the Major Leagues. In June 1978, I was drafted by the Baltimore Orioles in the third round. I had no idea the Orioles were even looking my way. I was in touch with the Yankees and the Cardinals and had my hopes set on one day playing for the Yanks. Brooks Robinson was one of my idols of the game along with Micky Mantle and Roberto Clemente, and I had spent hours playing games with them in my mind as I threw the ball against a wall. I developed quickly getting the ball out of my glove by making a glove from plywood. Yes, that's right: wood. I would throw a golf ball against the cement wall or steps, and as the ball would hit the wood on my hand, I would take the ball in my throwing hand and lob it back at the wall. This particular drill helped with my quickness and hand-eye coordination.

I loved the game so much, which involved competition not only against other players but against myself, trying to be the very best I could be. I rubbed a lot of dirt on my injuries and always got back in the game. But as hard as I practiced and played the game, I was equally intense when it came to drinking and partying.

On the outside, everything seemed great, but on the inside I was miserable. Living such a lie. As the battle raged in my mind and in my heart, it was getting even more difficult to deal with what was going on inside of me.

After I signed on with the Orioles, I was sent directly to Bluefield West Virginia where they had their Rookie Ball League. I spent about three weeks there and was then sent to Charlotte, North Carolina to finish out my first year of pro ball in the Southern League.

After a few games, I was injured on a play that almost ruined my career. I had a collision with a left fielder and landed on my hip. The force of hitting the ground severed one of the nerves in my lower back. My legs went numb. The trainer popped my dislocated hip back into place while I was still on the field and the sensation came back almost immediately. I stayed in the game and the next player hit a ball in the hole. As I planted my foot to catch the ball, my hip went out again and I collapsed with excruciating pain along my left side. I was helped off the field and spent much of that first summer in rehab, getting worked on every day by our trainer, Old Doc Cole, a retired chiropractor.

I thank the Lord for Doc Cole. If it weren't for him, I doubt I would ever have played again. However, the rehab was one of the most painful experiences in my life. Doc would work on my back every day for hours, tape me up, walk me to the field, and make me run from foul pole to foul pole. Every time my left foot hit the ground, pain would shoot and tears would flow as I ran each lap. Being a lost man, I had a few choice words for Doc each and every day. I am glad he put up with the verbal abuse I was giving him. I still had to travel with the club on long bus rides where I could sit down, but later had to stand for hours in pain. So my life was a battle with pain. It was a competition within my mind over just how much pain I could endure. I would pop pain pills during the day and at night drink myself into a stupor just to try and sleep for a few hours as the pain was winning.

At the same time, my wife was pregnant with our second little girl and was experiencing a horrifying situation of her own. The baby was due the first week of October, but my wife started bleeding in June. The doctor said that Becky needed complete bed rest for the rest of the pregnancy. My mom and Becky's mom took turns staying with her throughout the summer as I was trying to heal myself and fight through my injury.

When I finally was able to play, I received a call in August that Becky, bleeding, was being rushed to the hospital. Both the baby and Becky were in danger.

I flew to Bryan, Texas and went directly to the hospital where the doctors and nurses were wheeling Becky into surgery. There was blood everywhere. Her placenta had burst and the baby had to be taken and flown to another town by helicopter. The doctors let me see Becky for just a few moments before they wheeled her into the operating room. She grabbed my hand and said, "God's got this. I have complete peace. I have rededicated myself to the Lord. I was backslidden for a long time, but I am a Christian and God is using this situation to get my attention. I am giving my life to Him, and our baby is the Lord's." As they took her into the OR and I waited for the outcome, I kept pondering what Becky had just told me. I concluded that Becky knew God, but there was no way that God could ever forgive someone like me. I resigned myself to the idea that even though I believed in God, He could never forgive me and I was bound for hell.

Becky spent several days recovering and our little baby girl, Krissy, was flown 90 miles away to another hospital which had much better infant care. For two weeks, it was touch and go with the doctor telling us that if she made it, she would probably need special care all her life. Becky kept reassuring me that God had this. She had promised God that she would serve

Jesus for the rest of her life if He would save Krissy and make her healthy.

I had just started feeling better from my injury and was ready to get back to the field of dreams. So I left Becky in the care of her mom and went to finish out the season. After I got back home, Becky was rejoicing in the fact that God had not only healed her but that Krissy was completely healed as well. Becky was reading her Bible, going to church whenever the doors were open, and turning our home into a house of prayer instead of letting me party with my friends and use the home for the devil. She would pour my alcohol down the drain, grind up my pot in the disposal, and tell me this was Jesus's home now. Talk about change. I would wake up some nights to Becky on her knees laying her hands on me while I slept, praying that God would save my soul and make our family whole. The more she prayed, the faster I ran. The more I drank and stayed away, the more she was committed to the battle for my soul.

In October 1978, I threw the car keys to Becky and told her I wanted a divorce. I sent her home to her family 200 miles away. In my eyes, my marriage was over. I was ready to just crash and burn. When Becky got home, her dad hugged her, gave her money, and said "Go back to your husband, and let's just pray." She returned and two weeks later she dragged me to church where I heard the gospel of Jesus Christ.

The old evangelist was preaching on hell. I believed in hell and knew that was where I was headed. But then he began to preach on why Jesus came—why God became flesh—to pay for the sins of anyone who was willing to repent, believe, ask, and receive Him by faith. I went down to the altar at the invitation, weeping and crying over my sin, calling on Jesus to save my rotten soul. And suddenly, after many years of battling, victory flooded my soul with such relief. I was born again that day; Jesus saved my soul and changed my life. It was all about the competition, and the Savior won. I have never gotten over what Jesus did for me that day. Not only that, but he had healed my wife and baby, restored my marriage, and gave me a love I never knew.

I just had to tell my friends. When I did, they didn't really want to listen. I was amazed that they didn't want what I had just experienced. I knew I needed to find people who had experienced what had happened to me so that they could encourage me in a new battle: the daily walk with God, fighting against this corrupt flesh which now houses the Spirit of God. I never knew the battle I would face in the war against the world, my flesh, and the devil's crew. But I thank God that I have the victory that is in Jesus Christ, the Son of God. I do not battle for victory; I battle FROM victory. I have read the end of the book, and we win!

I am not perfect—far from it. My life as a lost man brought pain not only for myself but others around me. I know God has given me forgiveness for all those sins, but to anyone I have hurt or wronged: please forgive me. If you do not know Christ, I pray that you may know Him and power of His resurrection, and that you would receive his peace and love into your heart.

I still make mistakes, still make some bad decisions, but I know whom I have believed and am persuaded that He will keep me in His hands. If you have never tried it God's way, try it. I have never regretted it.

The competition will still rage as long as I am in this earthly body. But God has given me the means to deliver that death blow to this old flesh. Each and every day, the desire to walk with God, to be filled with His Spirit, gives me the strength to live in the victory that Jesus has secured for all who believe. This looks like getting in the word of God daily, searching my heart to see if I am worshipping the Lord Jesus, walking in His steps, surrendering to His work, and serving Him no matter where I am.

Chapter Three
Seeking Truth

When I first got saved at the age of 22, I had very little knowledge of what a church was, let alone denominations and doctrine. I had no clue what to do next. Still being a pro ball player, our games were often on Sundays, so church was out, at least during the season. During this season, someone gave me a Living Bible paraphrase. In that first month of being saved I read the whole thing. Then someone gave me an NIV Bible. I read it through from cover to cover the next month. I repeated that for the next several months, visiting all kinds of churches, with no one to really guide and disciple me. I went to all kinds of churches: Methodist, Lutheran, Baptist, Charismatic, Pentecostal, Church of Christ, and even Roman Catholic. I thought they all believed the same thing. Because I never got grounded in a particular church or their set of dogma, I just read my Bible, praying, "Please, Lord, I want to know the truth, Your truth."

Someone gave me some Navigators material that dealt with Bible memorization. Each of the small index cards had a verse in the NIV on one side and the same verse in the KJV on the other. The only side I could memorize without making a mistake was the KJV side. Eventually I went to a Christian bookstore and asked the person working behind the desk if they had any KJV Bibles. I didn't even know the "KJ" stood for "King James" (though I knew the "V" was for "Version"). I remember the clerk telling me that the KJV was very difficult to read and tried to steer me to another version, one that was easier to read. I told the young man, "No, I want a KJV." We dusted off the Bible and I bought my first KJV Bible, and then got a little pocket-sized KJV New Testament to carry with me wherever I went, even in my back pocket at spring training with the Orioles.

So, I began my journey in truth. The word became alive to me; it was all I wanted. But I knew I was missing out of the fellowship that was needed. I began to look for a church. I would take notes on every message I heard preached, go home and study, and found out that many of them were not lining up with the what the word was telling me.

In 1980, I was called up to Rochester, NY—home of the Rochester Red Wings, the farm club of the Orioles at the time. After a few days, I was interviewed and gave my testimony of how the Lord Jesus saved me and changed my life from doing drugs and alcoholism. Churches began to call for me to come and give my testimony. There was one young 14-year-old young man, Pete M., who tried to be at all the home games. He would yell at me the whole game, especially during practice, giving me information about his church nearby: First Bible Baptist Church. He kept begging me and telling me how great the church was and that the word was preached there; they even preached from the KJV. So I went, and man the light went on. The truth was not only being preached, but it was being lived out through evangelism, Bible studies, small groups, bus ministry, sports ministries. In time, Mike Metzger and his wife Louise came into our lives, loved us, and nurtured and discipled us in God's word. For so long I'd prayed, "God, I want to know the truth." My prayer became, "Lord, help me live the truth," and eventually, "Lord, help me give the truth."

There are so many problems that we are facing in the church today. Anxiety, fear, defeat, and much confusion and a battle over truth. Jesus said in John 17:17, "Sanctify them through thy truth; thy word is truth."

It seems the old devil has not stopped trying to confuse us or get us to doubt what God says in His word. The competition has been going on ever since the fall of Lucifer. Satan wants to do all he can to get the believer away from truth, to doubt it, to be confused as to whether we have the word of God with us today.

When King David got depressed by all the battles he was facing, he turned to God, prayed, and God gave him His word to bind up his broken and contrite spirit.

There is one thing I have learned about truth: God is NOT obligated to reveal truth to anyone who does not want it. There's the old saying: "You can lead a horse to water, but you can't make it drink." It can be similarly said, "You can lead a lost person to truth, but you can't make them think." Only God Himself can illuminate their minds and hearts if they want to know it. What a battle we face today. The battle is not really with the lost. We are commanded to tell them, whether they hear or not. It is often the "professing" Christian who seems to have a hard time finding truth.

Contrary to what people say today, there is no need for any additional revelation or words of prophecy. God's word is true. I have personally spent over 1000 hours studying just where our Bibles that we have today come from. If something is not absolute truth, then it is corrupt. Truth cannot be truth with any error in it. What fellowship has light with darkness?

I have spent much time talking with pastors and discussing the word of God and its infallibility. Our conversations always go back to, "Well, in the originals it says this or that." I try to remind them that we have NO originals today. All we have are copies of copies of copies of extant manuscripts, old versions, and the writings of the early church fathers and their beliefs. Many say you must know the Greek and Hebrew because the originals were written in those languages. Some even say that Latin is a must.

Defining your terms is so important when distinguishing between truth and error. It seems over the years that the meanings of words have changed. God's word does not change, but the way people talk about it does.

Have you ever heard the person say that only the "originals" are inspired? We have to ask, what is the meaning of inspiration? There are only two times in the Bible where the word "inspiration" occurs. One in the Old Testament and one in the New Testament. There is a principle when it comes to studying the Bible called the law of first mention. Let us look at the first time "inspiration" appears in the Bible.

Job 32:8 says, "But there is a spirit in man; and the inspiration of the Almighty giveth them understanding."

The Bible's first use of the word "inspiration" is the act of God getting understanding to the spirit of man. It doesn't have to do with original manuscripts.

The other mention of the word is in 2 Timothy 3:16, which says, "All scripture is given by inspiration of God, and is profitable for doctrine, for reproof, for correction, for instruction in righteousness:"

If we believe that God breathed and spoke creation, why do we think it is impossible that this same Almighty God could not preserve His word for us today?

Rather than seeking something more than God's revelation, we as believers need to study and obey what we already know. Remember, the Holy Spirit did not die with the originals. Why can't we just allow the scriptures to interpret themselves for us? Let the word define the word. Compare scripture with scripture and allow the Holy Spirit of God to give you that understanding.

Scripture has not failed us. Truth has not failed us. We have failed it. Because of our sinful neglect of not reading and studying and searching for God's truth, doctrinal confusion and lack of spiritual power inhabit the church today. Many have abandoned the truth for what the world is saying.

There is no substitute for submission to the scripture. Our spiritual health depends on it. We have traded the truth of God for a lie. Remember, God is not obligated to reveal truth to anyone who does not desire it.

There is no question that the church, our country, and our society today are under attack. We are in such a state of moral and spiritual decline. Truth is slandered and the lie is promoted. We are facing attacks on our Christian values, and because we are not standing up for the truth, our children and grandchildren are being exposed to what is coming. Where is our culture going? What kind of value system, what kind of morality, what kind of world is coming?

The world has an agenda, and more and more professing Christians are joining their ranks. They are aggressive, angry, and determined to impose that agenda on the rest of society. Society rejected biblical truth many years ago.

Many years ago, when I was playing ball, I would have to go and represent the Orioles at functions. A man with his son came up to me holding a scotch in his hand and said, "Bobby, don't you think it is horrible that big league ball players who drink and do drugs are setting terrible examples for our children?" I told him I thought that was terrible, but then I said to him, "Please do not put the burden on me of raising your child. If he turns out to be a drunk, he will not have far to look." He went away a little mad. We become who we follow. Follow Jesus, His word and not our private interpretation of the word.

It is amazing how our backbones today have gotten soft. It seems we cannot have a biblical view on anything. We are called to walk in God's word, to proclaim that His word is true and that there is no private interpretation of it. And yet many in the church are tolerant of sin rather than desiring holiness. The Bible says that "open rebuke is better than secret love" (Pro 25:5). So let's rub some dirt on it and get back in the game, because it is about the competition: the battle of truth versus lies, good versus evil, right versus wrong. As soon as "religion" or "politics" are mentioned we get our feathers ruffled.

Under the leading of the Holy Ghost, King David wrote many of the psalms. In Psalm 19, the scripture offers the faithful testimony of God Himself on the all-sufficiency of His word in every situation that comes into our lives.

The word "Lord" is used many times in Psalm 19. The law of the Lord... the testimony of the Lord... the statutes of the Lord... the commandment of the Lord... the fear of the Lord... the judgments of the Lord... David wanted the reader to know that scripture proceeds from God Himself. And each of these statements concerning His word describes its effect in the life of the person who believes and embraces it to be the truth.

In verse 7, the scripture says that the law of the Lord is perfect, converting the soul. There is no mention of culture or nation here. The word is everything that is necessary for one's spiritual life. Scripture is so powerful that it can convert or change or transform the entire person. God's word is so powerful it can change anyone, anywhere.

Truth provides a foundation upon which we build our lives and eternal destinies. Scripture is unwavering, immovable, unmistakable, reliable, and worthy to be trusted. So many are distracted and discouraged because they lack direction and purpose for their lives. Most seek answers from the wrong sources. The truth stands and does not waver or fade. We need a GPS: God's Positional System, aka His word!

There is no grey area when it comes to truth. Truth is absolute. Opinions are just what they are: opinions. Everyone has them. God's word is truth, with no lies, no errors. The word of God is without sin, evil, corruption, or error. Scripture endures forever. It is eternally perfect. The Bible is permanent, unchanging, and relevant to everyone in every age of history.

Are we anxious, fearful, doubting? Learn to obey God's word and begin to share in the joy that is divine. Stop turning to self-help programs and pursuits. Focus on divine truth. Only there we will find true joy. God's word is not a bunch of suggestions. They are not optional or an additive to help along the way.

The Bible stands in contrast to the world's system. Those who do not seek truth will end up believing a lie. They become blind and unable to discern truth.

Do you desire truth? Do you want to know the purpose of life? To know what is moral, what to value? Do you know how to answer questions like, "What is my destiny? Is hell real? Where can I find love? Hope? Security? What about every issue of life?"

What a privilege to possess the word of truth. God's word satisfies our spiritual hunger. There is no substitute for submission to truth. Are we trading divine power for temporal moments of self-satisfaction? If so, rub some dirt on it and get back in the game!

Chapter Four
I Got Traded

In December 1983, after the Orioles won the World Series, I received a phone call from the front office that I would not be receiving a World Series Ring, even though they had measured me for one. Then they told me that my contract would be cut and I would be sent back to the Minor League. I was shocked, hurt, disheartened. I asked to be traded. They told me that they wouldn't get anyone in exchange for me—I wasn't worth a trade. I responded with, "If I'm not worth anything, then give me an unconditional release so I can sign with whomever." They said no. I was so angry that I had been lied to and rejected. I went to the back of the house and opened my Bible right to John 21. Peter had gone back to his profession as a fisherman even after he had seen the resurrected Jesus on two other occasions, and now Jesus showed up for the third time. Jesus asked Peter three times if he loved him more than fishing. Fishing was his livelihood; baseball was mine. It meant everything to me, and God was speaking to me in my heart, "Bobby, do you love baseball more than me?" I began to make excuses to the Lord: "Look what I've done for you. I've given up everything for you. I have been a witness for you since I got saved."

There was a struggle going on in my soul. I realized that baseball was indeed a god in my life. I made a vow to the Lord that I would go back and finish my last year in the Minor Leagues and give each game to Jesus. Then I would be a free agent and the trade on my life would be complete and I could walk away from baseball to serve the Lord wherever He decided.

I had the greatest year and four major league clubs called to offer me a contract. I was 28 years old, in the prime of my life, and finally understood what it meant to be a utility player after having been a starter all my life. I now had the experience and patience to play the game. But I decided to walk away and serve the Lord full-time wherever He wanted me. He had won.

I have never once regretted my decision to walk away from the diamond. I have never gotten over Jesus saving my soul and placing His robe of righteousness and His garment of salvation and garment of praise on this needy sinner.

The competition continues as I battle this old flesh; it is corrupt and does not want to serve God. The battle also continues with this old world, which hates the believer in Jesus Christ. The battle against the devil is also real as he whispers in our ears about how we are unworthy. The Bible calls him the "accuser of the brethren" (Rev 12:10). Shame comes from the devil; conviction comes from God.

Stop listening to the enemies: the world, the flesh, and the devil. It is a competition, but we wrestle not against flesh and blood, but against spiritual wickedness in high places (Eph 6:12). If that old devil has been telling you that you are worthless and no good, just rub some dirt on it and get back in the game.

The Orioles told me I was worth nothing in a trade. But I had already made the greatest trade of all time years before:

I traded my sins for Jesus's righteousness.

Jesus took the suffering—I got to go free.

Jesus was stripped naked—He clothed me in righteousness.

Jesus was put to death—I was born again.

Jesus became a curse—I received blessings.

Galatians 3:13 Christ hath redeemed us from the curse of the law, being made a curse for us: for it is written, Cursed is every one that hangeth on a tree: 14 That the blessing of Abraham might come on the Gentiles through Jesus Christ; that we might receive the promise of the Spirit through faith.

It is by His grace that we are redeemed. We are offered a garment of freedom, and one size fits all! Lord, help us to walk and live a life that is worthy of the robe of righteousness that You have placed upon us by faith.

Thank you for the blood that has redeemed my soul and allowed me to have a relationship with You, King Jesus!

Have you ever been told you're worthless or that nobody wants you? Well, Jesus wants you! God says He is not willing that any should perish, but that all should come to repentance (2Pe 3:9). Why not trade your sins right now for His righteousness? Believe that Jesus died for our sins according to the scriptures, was buried, and rose again the third day according to the scriptures (1Co 15:1-4). Call upon Him to save you, and He will. It will be the greatest trade of your life.

If you don't know how to pray, below is an example prayer. But the real question is: do you want the trade? Do you want to be born again? Do you want an eternal place in Heaven one day? Do you want your sins washed away?

Here is the simple prayer:

Dear God,

I know that I am a sinner and that there is nothing I can do to earn salvation. I know that you love me and sent your Son Jesus to die on the cross for me. I believe that He rose from the dead, and right now I am calling on You to forgive my sins. Save my soul!

Thank you for hearing my prayer. Amen.

If you sincerely prayed something like the above, then you got put on the best team ever! You have been traded from going to hell to heaven, from walking in darkness to walking in light. Not only that, but it is an eternal contract! This is just the beginning of your new life. Read your Bible and pray every day, find a good Bible-believing church and plug in, and share Jesus with all.

If you prayed to receive Jesus Christ as your Savior after reading this book, please contact me and let me know! To God be the glory.

If you want to learn how to compete and have spiritual victory no matter the score, stop saying, "Woe is me," and shout, "Wow is He!"

Chapter Five

Seeking God's Face

A few weeks before the baseball season ended in 1984, I met with Pastor Grace, and he was asking me about my future. What was I going to be doing after the last game? I told him I had not decided and was looking into possibly entering the ministry. As we talked, he asked, "How would you like to work at NCA as a teacher and coach?" NCA was Northstar Christian Academy, a Christian school that was a ministry of our church. Since that was the only job offer I received, I said yes. So after playing a double header on a Sunday in September, the next day I showed up at the school to start my first day. I was so excited. Pastor Grace created a job and ministry for me. I poured my time and effort into the school, the students, and a brand-new team.

I got up at 5 a.m. every morning, studied, then headed off to school Monday through Friday, all day teaching a handful of subjects, plus coaching after school. I would get home around 7 p.m. unless there was a nighttime game; then it was usually midnight by the time I got home. On certain nights, I would attend the Bible institute in the evening. On Saturdays, we had a men's prayer meeting early, bus visitation, and door-to-door evangelism. On Sundays, I left early around 7 a.m. to pick up local kids for Sunday school and then taught them in class, returned them home after church, and got home myself around 3 or 4 in the afternoon. Then I headed back to church for Sunday evening service. Whew! Are you tired yet? And of course, all the while I had a wife and children to minister to. Wow! Busy, busy, busy to say the least.

A couple years went by with this weekly schedule. There was a man in our church named Ronnie who came to me and asked me to meet him at church at 11:30 on Monday night. I asked what for. He said, "Bobby, let's pray all night!" I told Ronnie that I had never prayed for more than an hour. I explained to him my schedule, how I was barely sleeping as it was and just did not have any time. Ron asked me when I got saved; I told him when I was 22. He asked, "Before you got saved, did you stay up all night for the devil and his crowd?"

Conviction flooded my soul as I remembered all those nights of staying up all night drinking and drugging. I told him yes, I did. Then he asked me a second question: "Bobby, do you like to fish? Do you like to hunt?" I told him I did. He asked, "Did you ever stay up all night to hunt or fish, satisfying your flesh?" Hunting and fishing are not sinful, but it was what I loved to do. I answered yes, with even more conviction that flooded my soul. He went on to say, "So you stayed up all night for the devil and his crowd, you stayed up all night to fulfill your flesh, but you won't try to stay up all night to seek God's face?" Filled with conviction, I looked up at Ron and said, "I'll meet you at church at 11:30 on Monday night."

When I got home, I told Becky of our conversation, and she of course was initially worried about my physical health. But in her spirit knew it would be okay. What is wrong with sacrificing time and sleep to seek God's face, His person, His direction?

Monday morning came. I was up early off to work, taught, coached, went home, went to the church for Bible institute classes, then came back home and spent some time with the family. At 11:00 p.m., I kissed Becky and met Ronnie at the church at 11:30 that night like I'd promised.

Ronnie and I went down to the altar with our Bibles, got on our knees, would read the word for a few minutes, and then pray according to what we were hearing from the Scriptures. We prayed for our pastor, the church staff, their spouses and children, our families, local government, senators, the President, our missionaries, and each and every member of our church. In between these prayers, we would sing a psalm or a hymn, read some more of the word and praise our God for His goodness, mercy, grace, and love. We thanked Him for everything, enjoying our time in the word, worship, and the wonder of our King Jesus. The next thing we knew, the sun was coming up around 6:00 a.m.

I went home took a shower, had a quick bite to eat, and headed off for my regular weekly schedule. But each Monday night, Ronnie and I would meet and pray all night.

After a month or so, a group of men in our church heard about what we were doing, and they began to join us. It is amazing what can happen when we seek the face of God, just desiring His presence in our midst. We had no idea what the Lord was going to do in our lives. We just wanted to know Him, to pursue the One who gave His eternal life. What a journey. We continued meeting each week for several months, and God began to move in all of our hearts. In time, God called each of those men to go somewhere in this world and be a part of the ministry of Jesus Christ.

We did not have a program. We just wanted a person: the Lord Jesus Christ. We wanted to know Him. And in pursuing Him, we each found a place that he wanted us to be. But it all started with the word, which moved us to worship, which was followed by a walk. Then, God allowed us to be involved in His work, and chose many different places where we would serve Him.

There is a big difference between seeking God's Face and seeking His hands — the person of Jesus Christ versus His provisions. Often, we desire the gifts more than the gift-giver. We are not afraid to ask God for just about anything it seems. But what about the request of seeing His face?

> *Psalm 27:4 One thing have I desired of the LORD, that will I seek after; that I may dwell in the house of the LORD all the days of my life, to behold the beauty of the LORD, and to enquire in his temple. ... 8 When thou saidst, Seek ye my face; my heart said unto thee, Thy face, LORD, will I seek.*

I am afraid that sometimes the reason we don't seek the Lord with all our hearts and minds is because the Lord is LIGHT. There is no darkness in Him. When we get close to the Lord, His light shines and manifests the dark spots in our lives that we're trying to hide, exposing our hypocrisies, our pride, our stubbornness, our secret sins.

There is nothing wrong with asking God for things, for His provision. There's nothing wrong with seeking His Hands. But is that all we do? Let us seek the Lord, let us knock on His door until He answers, let us ask the Lord according to His will. I don't think there will be anyone in hell who said, I sought You, Lord; where were You? Lord, I knocked; why didn't You open?

A few years ago, after returning from Africa, my oldest Daughter told me about some books that Daniel Henderson had written about prayer. She sent them to me. As I read them, I cried and praised God for not only showing Ronnie and the gang of men at our church this truth, but now in revealing it to my daughter as well.

One final point regarding seeking God's face and presence are the four "Laws of Marriage." From the beginning, God established four powerful principles for marriage, found in Genesis 2:24-25. While these biblical principles apply directly to a husband and wife, they can also be applied to Jesus and our relationship with him as part of the Church, the Bride of Christ.

1. The Law of Priority

Get your life in order. Stop competing and fighting for things that are going to all be burnt up or turned over to someone else. Put God first in your life. Make the commitment to seek His face. When asked which was the greatest commandment, what was Jesus's response? To love the Lord with all your heart, soul, mind, and strength (Mark 12:29-30).

What is your priority? Is God first in your life? Or are you allowing temporal things to win the battle over your attention?

2. The Law of Pursuit

Genesis 2:24 uses the word "cleave," which is translated in other parts of the Bible as "follow" or "pursue". Are we pursuing God's presence? Matthew 6:33 says, "But seek ye first the kingdom of God, and his righteousness; and all these things shall be added unto you." What are you seeking after? Are you seeking or cleaving to physical things, or are you seeking God and His work and allowing Him to work out the rest?

3. The Law of Possessions

We have been bought with a price: the precious blood of Jesus Christ. When we hold onto things and deny the Lord access to everything we have, we break this law. Do we really trust the Lord in and with everything? Is what's ours His? Anything we do not allow the Lord to have a part of becomes an idol in our lives. Our very lives are not even our own; we are Christ's.

4. The Law of Purity

It says in Genesis that Adam and Eve were naked and not ashamed. Similarly, there is nothing between us and our Savior. He sees us for all that we are and loves us. But do we live in this freedom, or are we busy covering our shame of idleness and unfruitfulness?

The Lord knows the secret places. The Lord knows all about our battles with the flesh and pride. What we need is some openness with Jesus, looking into that perfect law of liberty, searching our hearts to see if there anything in there that needs to come out. If there is something that needs cleansed, what's the answer? In Ephesians 5, the Bible tells us that Christ washes His Bride with the water of His word.

Don't just seek God's hand. Ask for your needs, but remember that He already knows them and has promised to provide. Seek His face, and you will find all the fulfillment you could ever need and more.

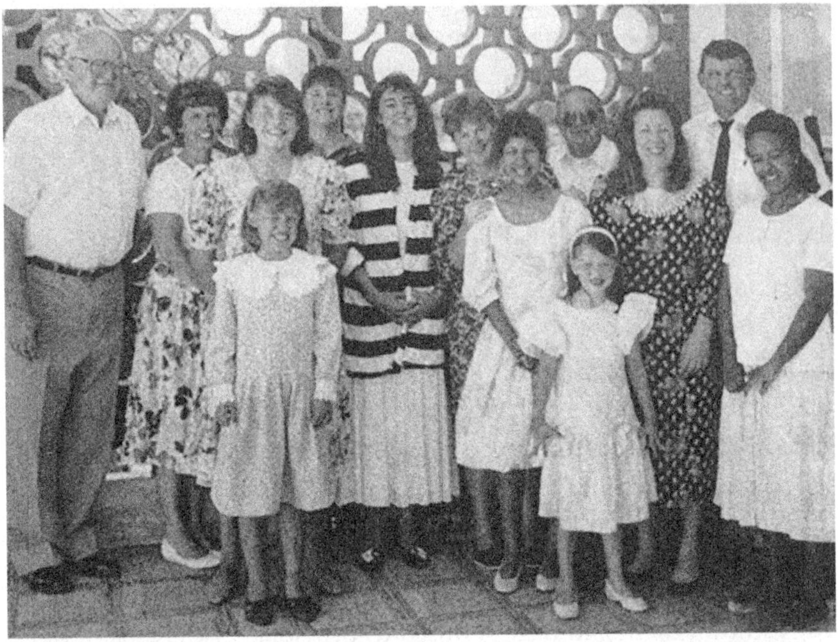

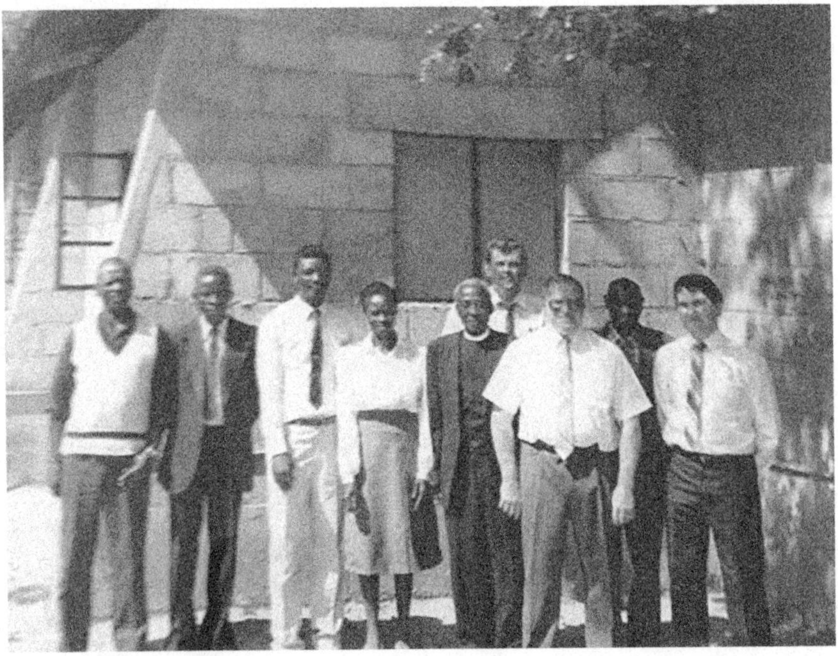

Chapter Six
Being Sent

In 1986, a veteran missionary came to our church and spoke on the need for missions in Africa. As he spoke, I remembered the day back in 1983 when I realized that baseball had become a god in my life. I'd been so convicted at the time. I'd made a deal with God that after I finished out the season, even if he wanted me to go to Africa, I would go.

Of course, as time goes by, we tend to forget the commitments we make to God. But as that missionary spoke about Africa, I went forward and surrendered to go. As I got up from the altar, another man in our church stood up and said God was calling him to Africa. I thought, "Wow! He just told everyone. Now he has to go!" I thought for a moment that maybe I overheard God calling my friend instead of me, so I just kept my mouth closed and did not tell anyone. Every day after that, I could not get over what I had told God and how He was daily reminding me of the commitment I had made to Him. In everything I read, everything I heard, day after day, night after night, conviction flooded my soul. I had to go.

I told my wife and she was shocked, but she was willing to follow me anywhere. We had just started a ministry at our church called The Bobby Bonner Summer Sports Program. I went in to talk to my pastor to tell him I was surrendering to go to Africa. I thought he would be excited, but he wasn't. He said, "God has not called you to Africa. He would have told me. We just started this program to reach our community with sports and you're a big part of it." I assured him that God was indeed calling me. He assured me that God was not calling me. As I left his office, I was perplexed to say the least.

Here was a man of God whom I loved and respected more than any other man, and he was telling me that God had not called me to Africa. The more I thought about it, the angrier I got. How could he see my heart? How could he know all the sleepless nights, prayers, the vow I had made? So I decided to go in again and meet with him and tell him all that God had been showing me since 1983.

In the meeting, my pastor said once again that God had not called me to Africa. As I was leaving his office, I said, "If I don't go, I am going to die. So I am going with or without your blessing." I turned to go. My pastor asked me to come back in and shut the door. He then said to me, "Bobby, if I could talk you out of going, then God would not be in it." We then sat down and prayed, and he helped me get started with a plan on how to get there. I thank God for my pastor. A good pastor or shepherd will not only challenge you but recognize the Lord working in your heart.

I remember starting deputation—the missionary term for fundraising—and my first 100 phone calls were all the same: "What missions board? What church? Never heard of you, sorry." A hundred answers, all the same: "No." Man, was God really in this? I went to my pastor and told him what happened. He asked, "Did you mention you're a former baseball player?" I said no. He said try again.

In the very next call I made, I told the pastor my history of playing Major League baseball, and I got a meeting. It seemed like from then on it was a yes. In competition, always look for the edge. It worked.

I was on deputation for a little over 10 months. Sunday morning, Sunday night, Saturday baseball clinics with evangelism, during the week, meeting with pastors for breakfast, lunch, Wednesday night meetings, Thursday night meetings. Pastors introducing me to other pastors, preaching at different Bible colleges like Midwestern Baptist College under the leadership of Dr. Tom Malone. I went wherever the door was opened, just trusting the Holy Spirit to lead and guide me. From Maine to Florida, New York to California, Texas to Alaska, I put in over 100,000 miles in less than a year.

For years, I have watched missionaries at missions conferences do their best to catch the pastor's eye or ear, jockeying for position and provision. I can understand that and really have no problem with it. I just believe that if God is in it—and if you are in the word, truly worshipping Him in spirit and in truth, and walking with Him in obedience to His commands—then the work becomes His work, and He will supply the resources to get the job done!

> *Hebrews 11:1 Now faith is the substance of things hoped for, the evidence of things not seen. 2 For by it the elders obtained a good report. 3 Through faith we understand that the worlds were framed by the word of God, so that things which are seen were not made of things which do appear. 4 By faith Abel offered unto God a more excellent sacrifice than Cain, by which he obtained witness that he was righteous, God testifying of his gifts: and by it he being dead yet speaketh. 5 By faith Enoch was translated that he should not see death; and was not found, because God had translated him: for before his translation he had this testimony, that he pleased God. 6 But without faith it is impossible to please him: for he that cometh to God must believe that he is, and that he is a rewarder of them that diligently seek him. 7 By faith Noah, being warned of God of things not seen as yet, moved with fear, prepared an ark to the saving of his house; by the which he condemned the world, and became heir of the righteousness which is by faith.*

However, I do know a little bit about life as a missionary here in the USA, traveling around, becoming—if not careful—a "moochinary" instead of trusting in the Lord to supply our every need.

Our time of deputation—traveling all around, going from church to church presenting our field, our burden, our call, and what we would be doing once we got to the field—was a wonderful time of learning. Some call it the dog and pony show: looking good, saying the right things, doing all the things expected, hoping your kids will behave and not tell any secrets about what mommy and daddy do or say. We had a wonderful experience for the most part.

However, every missionary has a few horror stories. Once when visiting a pastor in West Virginia, he asked me to come to preach and present the work. Way up in the hills, out in the sticks as they say, I stayed with the pastor at his house. He had a two-bedroom house, one bathroom, and five kids ages 4 to 12 who all slept in one bedroom with the wife and pastor in the other. They put me on an army cot in the hallway between the bedrooms with paper thin walls. Use your imagination. Yes, it was that bad. I left the next morning with little sleep and glad to be back on the road.

Another time, I went to a church in Detroit and preached for a pastor who then took me to the hotel I would be staying at. It was one of those red-light, rent by the hour places if you know what I mean. I left and drove down the road and got another hotel on my own. Several times during deputation I just slept on the side of the road at a rest stop and bathed out of the sink the next morning. It was good experience, especially in preparation for the places I would be staying at when I got to the African bush.

Every missionary I've met, maybe apart from a couple, always says the same thing: we are going to the field to win souls, plant churches, and train nationals to take over churches. However, over time, the results differ. They don't wind up doing what they set out to do, yet they still rely on the financial support of churches in the USA. I have no problem with you receiving help from the brethren back home; just be sure to hold up your end of the bargain and do the work you agreed to do. Don't think that just because you're in a foreign field you are entitled to their support. The only thing we deserve is hell; we're not entitled to anything.

If we are truly called by Him, then He will take care of us, because it's His work! Once again, this is not a condemnation of what others have done or are doing. My observations are just that: my observations. All in all, I understand that every missionary who is born again is my brother in Christ. They are not my enemy, but a fellowlaborer in the Lord's work. Most of my encounters with other missionaries have been a blessing to say the least. I am so encouraged that others are listening and surrendering to the Spirit's call.

Early in our ministry in Africa, we were the only independent Baptist church in the country. There were plenty of other groups in the country, but no independent Baptists. I was praying every day for workers, for more missionaries to come, because the fruit was ripe. People's hearts were open to truth. I helped other groups get into the country even though they were from different missions boards. Some were coming from different countries in Africa after being chased out. They were an answer to my prayer. Yet despite these blessings, criticism came from the brethren: "How can you fellowship with this or that group?" I could not believe the schism I was seeing, even among independent Bible-believing churches. And then, once I'd helped them get established in the country, it seemed the independence once again set in, and the competition was on.

One thing I learned a long time ago is that the work was never my work; it is God's. I am called to be a servant, a steward of the manifold grace of God. The brethren are not my enemy.

After serving in Africa a few years, coming back to the US was much easier. I had some experience under my belt and had learned how to trust the Lord even when I was out of sight of our supporters. I was living by faith. Furlough was and has always been fun to me.

On one particular trip home, another man asked if he could join me on some of my trips to different churches to learn how this deputation works as he had just surrendered to go to a foreign country. We went to one very large church, and after the service all the missionaries went to someone's home to fellowship with pastors from all over the country. My friend asked me to show him how to talk to a pastor and try and get a meeting. We approached a pastor from Maryland and, after introducing ourselves to him, I asked if I could come and present the work in Africa to his church. He said he was sorry that he already had that spot covered as they supported a family in Africa. He wanted to have a missionary on each continent, he said. I was going to ask him who he supported in Antarctica, but did not. But I did ask him if he was a baseball fan. His face lit up; he was a huge Orioles fan and Cal Ripken was his favorite player. I then told him I played with the Orioles and Cal was my roommate one year. He immediately changed his attitude from "don't talk to me" to begging me to come to his church and preach, and maybe we could take in a game and maybe meet some players. He went on and on. As he asked us to plan a date, I told him I was busy and could not come to his church. My buddy just sat there with his mouth open. I thought it was funny. A few years later I went to his church, but they never supported me. I should have changed my field to Antarctica.

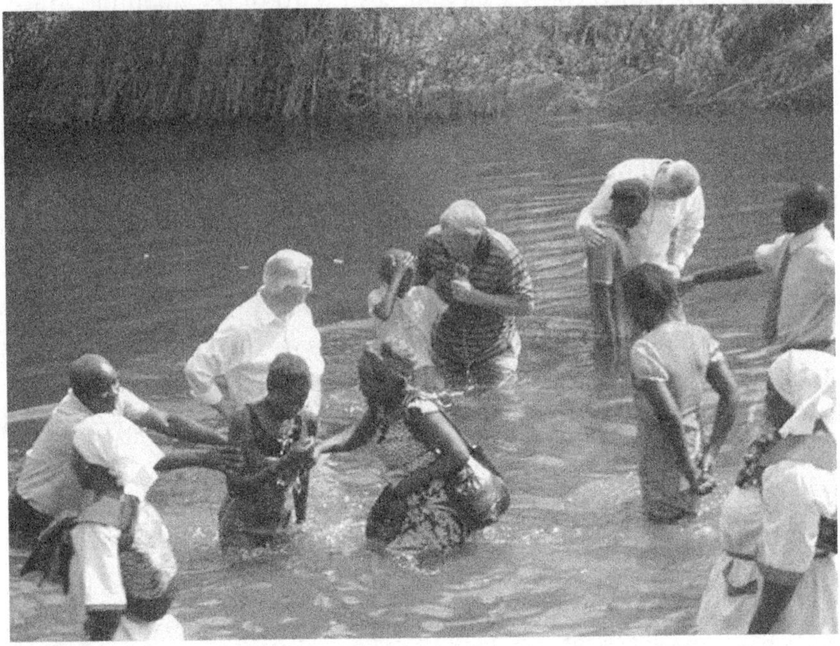

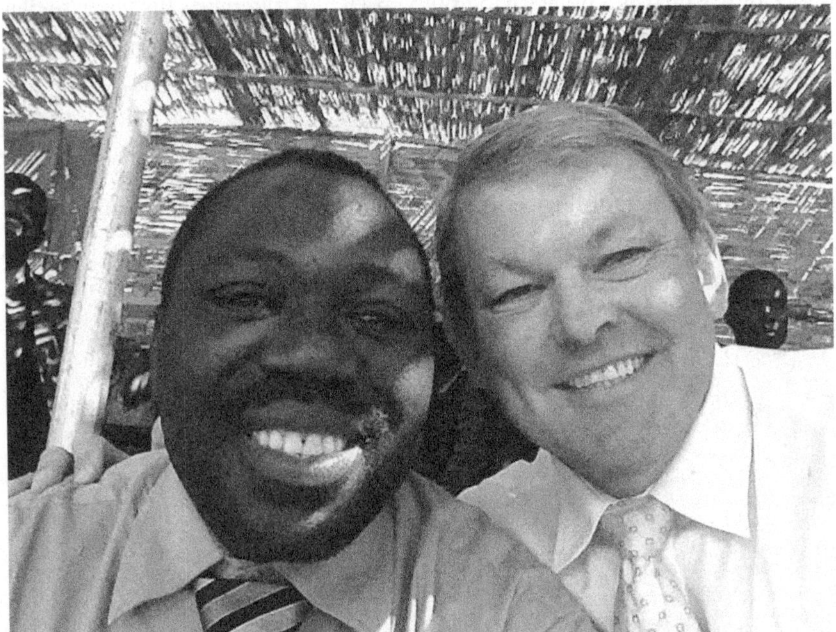

Chapter Seven

Zambia

Culture is a powerful thing. It's made up of the customs, arts, social institutions, and achievements of a particular group and is learned over time.

If you move someone from one culture to another, especially as a young person, there is often a clash. I have seen that here in the USA when a child has been adopted from another country. If they're old enough, they come here with customs and achievements from that particular nation, but as they grow up in the States they become a part of a new culture. Sometimes they "relearn" how to live according to their new culture, but some never assimilate and feel left out or different.

In today's world, there are so many battles of culture. There are battles to change traditions, enter a new age of belief, with all kinds of social changes going on even within particular groups of people who would claim they agree with each other. People say things like, "That's so old-fashioned... We no longer live in that time... Times have changed, and we should change with the times."

But throughout time and culture, there is only ONE thing that does not change, and that is GOD. His holiness does not change, the way to Him does not change, and His word does not change. His way is narrow and His word is authoritative and true. Humanity is trying to change the definition of truth, but God says that His word is truth (John 17:17).

When Becky and I and the kids first arrived in Zambia many years ago, it was new to say the least. We had left our western culture for a much different one. Food, music, language, worship, social activity, and even ways of thinking were very different. Even the usage of terms and definitions of words were different. I remember once, before all of our belongings arrived, I needed some tools around the house and went out looking for a crescent wrench—at least, that's what my dad called it growing up. Every store I went in did not have a crescent wrench, but they had a shifting spanner. Different names for different tools!

The first year was the hardest. Communication and understanding the culture was so foreign. I can remember crying out to God, praying, "Lord, they don't understand me. Please help them to understand me." As I prayed that prayer day upon day, God eventually showed me that it was never their responsibility to understand me; it was mine to understand them. How they thought, how they lived, how they dealt with life and death and daily living. Boy, was my world turned around almost immediately.

Within days of praying this over and over, I contracted cerebral malaria, which has a 95% fatality rate. I was placed in a local hospital there, basically getting ready to see my Maker. But by a miracle, I began to improve. My wife checked me out of the hospital and we learned to put IVs in ourselves. I survived, but God taught me a lesson as to just what the local people deal with every day and moved me to compassion.

As we opened a little health center in the bush, scores of people would come in for malaria treatment, many of whom were HIV positive. As I watched the suffering and pain of loss—especially of little children—I became overwhelmed that the message of the gospel must be preached all over as soon as possible, as so many were dying without Jesus Christ. So we went from village to village, town to town, preaching the gospel message. We saw many people come to Christ. Churches were being planted, men being trained, and the Great Commission of Matthew 28 lived out day by day.

Nonetheless, language barriers, different terminology, and lack of understanding created some very frustrating times. I ran into one of these times at a Bible conference. During these conferences, many churches got together, picked a spot, and then spent weeks building a tabernacle out of the grass and trees, digging holes for makeshift toilets. At this specific conference, so many people showed up—several thousand—that we ran out of food, and the leaders came to me with the problem. I asked them for the nearest place to buy more supplies. They picked a guide to lead me and we took off. After about 30 minutes, I asked the guide how close we were. He responded, "Very near." After an hour of driving, I asked again; he said the same thing. As we drove and drove, the roads got smaller and smaller and civilization was getting further and further away with no fuel stations in sight. With my fuel tank closing in on the halfway point, I pulled over and asked, "Just how close is this place we are going to?" He once again said, "Very near." I explained our problem. If we kept going with no fuel stations where we were headed, we would not make it back to the conference. After traveling another 30 minutes, I pulled over and said to my guide, "Listen, your 'very near' and my 'very near' do not mean the same thing. Why do you keep telling me we're very near?" His response was, "I do not want to discourage you." We continued to travel and eventually got to our destination to buy food. As we started to head back, I knew the only way we were going to make it was if God somehow made our fuel last or if we found some fuel out here in the bush. All of a sudden, we noticed a small road with some buildings. I pulled in and was greeted by some South African farmers who had plenty of fuel. They shared with us and we were able to get back to the conference with the food. This was a learning experience.

On the lighter side, a group of women once came from Alabama to visit us and help with a church plant and VBS. As we were driving from the capital city of Lusaka back to the mission station, we passed through several police stops where they would sometimes ask for your license, maybe check the tires or tags to make sure everything was up to date. As we stopped at one of these checkpoints, I was driving four of the ladies in my little truck—a small four-door Isuzu Bakkie as they call it in South Africa. The policeman looked inside the vehicle and said, "Missionary, we are checking hooters today." When he said that, there were a couple of gasps and one of the women crossed her chest with her arms. I relayed that the hooter was the horn of the vehicle, honked it, and we went on our way. Cultural differences can at times be frustrating, but they can also be humorous.

Cultural differences are oftentimes so misunderstood that we don't even want to try to understand just where we are and who we are dealing with. In those early days, we went anywhere the Lord opened a door. When we got to a new area, proper protocol was to ask the chief for permission to even be there. They always allowed us to preach and evangelize.

I talked with a missionary who told me to be careful when talking to the chiefs, because many of them have multiple wives. He said if I witnessed to them and they got saved, they would want to be baptized. I told him that was wonderful. He responded by telling me that he would never baptize anyone who had more than one wife, because if he did then they would be a member of his church which did not allow multiple wives. I asked this missionary what the requirement for biblical baptism was. He responded, of course, that it is to be born again by faith in Jesus as Lord and Savior. But he restated that any of those chiefs could not be members of his church, so he would not baptize them.

I went back to the mission center and opened my Bible, asking the Lord to show me the truth. As I read Acts, I saw that people received the word of God, they got saved, and then they got baptized and continued in the doctrine of the church. But I had to then ask: what constitutes church membership? Is it having only one wife? I knew at the very least that according to 1 Timothy that a chief with multiple wives couldn't be a leader in the church.

I heard a story once of a missionary who led to the Lord a chief who had three wives, with children from each of the women. The chief made a profession of faith in Jesus and asked the missionary to baptize him, but the missionary refused, saying because he had more than one wife this was forbidden. After several months of begging this missionary to baptize him, he came to him once more and told him that he now only had one wife. The missionary asked the chief what happened to the other two. The chief smiled and said he had them executed. WOW. I wonder how the missionary responded to that.

According to scripture, being dunked in water does not place you into the membership of a local church. There are three steps I believe the early church used as a requirement for local church membership. Number one: a statement of one's salvation; that they are born again by grace through faith in the finished work of Jesus Christ, not their own works. Second: biblical immersion baptism after salvation. Third: agreeing with the doctrines of the particular church. After all, how can two walk together unless they agree (Amos 3:3)? The word of God must dictate our actions, not any religious culture.

The word says that we are baptized by the Spirit of God into one body, the body of Christ (1Co 12:13). However, in most local churches, not everyone is saved. There are some who are trusting works, some trusting in baptism, some trusting their own goodness. But anyone who places their faith in

Christ for salvation is baptized by the Spirit into his body.

When the Lord gave me peace about this, I began to witness to the chiefs. One chief I led to the Lord had three wives and children with each of them. He followed the Lord in baptism, and I had many opportunities to disciple him and share with him what the word said. Even though he was the chief in their community, I told him he could not be a deacon or a pastor. He took his first wife into his home to be his wife but built two other homes for the other two and their children. In their culture, those women and their children would starve if he sent them away. We never learned how to deal with that in Bible school. I am not sure if everything we did was precisely right, but we did try to follow the Lord and allow His word to speak and direct us. Our culture was the word of God.

Once, a precious deacon in one of our churches became very sick. He was from a very large village. I went to visit him several times, and he kept getting worse and worse. He finally mentioned that his grandmother had been bringing the witch doctor to try and heal him. I told him that going to the witch for healing was sin and that God was not pleased. He said he knew that but was so weak and was afraid to speak up against his grandmother, the matriarch of the family. I went to her and told her that going to the witch was against the word of God. She began to scream at me and called me a stupid *mzungu* (the Swahili equivalent for *honky*). She told me this was their culture and for me to go back to mine. I told her that as Christians we are not to go to the witches for anything, that it is an abomination to God, and that if her grandson died his blood would be on her. The word of God is to be the culture of the believer, no matter what country they are from. Witchcraft is a sin in American and Africa, and anywhere else it is practiced. A few days later, my dear brother went to Jesus. Amazingly, the family still asked me to preach his funeral. I pulled no punches, and that was the start of my battles against the witches and their power over the people we were called to minister to. Five witch doctors began to try and destroy me and my family. Praise the Lord, God protected us so many times—three of them were saved and began to serve in the ministry. That is the power of biblical culture!

Chapter Eight
Missionary vs. Missionary

We know that the words "missionary" and "missions" are not found in the Bible, but the command of being sent is. Every born-again believer has been sent to this world to be a witness of the glorious gospel of our Lord Jesus Christ. To tell the world the greatest message ever given. That God loves them and sent His only Son to give His life, to shed His blood for our sins. The sins that have separated us from God have now been washed away by the crimson flow. And after three days and three nights, Jesus rose from the dead and is now sitting at the right hand of the Father in Heaven. He is alive! What a message! What a Savior!

When Paul was writing to the Romans, he told them, "By whom we have received grace and apostleship, for obedience to the faith among all nations, for his name" (Rom 1:5). He said we that have received grace, and that those of us who were saved by that wonderful grace (Eph 2:8-9) have also received "apostleship".

The word apostle means "sent one". We are sent after we get saved to represent the Lord Jesus Christ wherever we go in this world. To our neighbors across the street, our families, our sphere of influence, however small or big that might be. We are all missionaries in that regard.

But there are those whom God seeks out and gets ahold of their hearts for something a little more adventurous, let's say: to take the gospel to the ends of the earth. To go to a different culture, a different country, a different community.

Missionaries come in many forms. Many different evangelical groups have foreign and domestic missionaries they train and support and send out. I am not familiar with all the different religious groups who send missionaries out into the world, so I can only speak of what I have personally experienced being sent out of a local, independent Baptist church. I was not affiliated or under any missions board. I was trained, discipled, and sent out of a local church to go and plant other churches. And even within the independent Baptist realm, there are differences when it comes to the ideology of missions. It does not mean they are right and I am wrong or vice versa. We are different, but hopefully all fulfilling the Great Command of our Lord.

Matthew 28:19 Go ye therefore, and teach all nations, baptizing them in the name of the Father, and of the Son, and of the Holy Ghost, 20 Teaching them to observe all things whatsoever I have commanded you: and, lo, I am with you alway, even unto the end of the world. Amen.

I remember one time at a missions conference in the USA, a local church which supported many missionaries around the world invited three of them from three different mission fields: one from Korea, one from Australia, and one from Africa (me). The church wanted to have veteran missionaries in, those who had been on the field for over 20 years at least. We were each given 15 minutes to talk about our work on the field and then to end with one urgent prayer request.

The first stood up and talked about his life in Korea and the work and then ended with his request that God would raise up a pastor to take over his work of pastoring a church on the field.

The second missionary, from Australia, stood up gave a wonderful report and ended with the same request, to please pray that God would raise up someone to take over his work of pastoring a local church on a foreign field.

I then stood up and told everyone that I do not pastor any works on the field. During my first two years on the field, I pastored 19 different churches—sixteen we re-established and three brand new works. I realized that I could not pastor that many all at the same time, so the Lord directed me to start a pastor-training curriculum to train African men to pastor African churches. After several years, those 19 churches started 19 more, and then we had 38, then 76, and today the nationals themselves are planting churches all over Sub-Saharan Africa, training their own people to reach their own people with the gospel of Jesus Christ. My prayer request was a little different; I asked the church to please pray about supporting our African church planters as they go and lead others to Jesus, disciple them, and train them to be pastors and church planters in the next village or town. Training Nationals to reach Nationals—TNT. It is dynamite!

When I finished, the pastor of the church asked all of us to go down to the front so people could come visit with and pray for us. I stood there all alone as most of those who came down went to the other two missionaries to talk with and pray for them. No one seemed to get what we were doing. Even the pastor of the church seemed to disappear when I was around the rest of the week. It was all about the competition, and it seemed we were playing in different leagues. There are several factors I believe go into this kind of reaction. One is that I was not from their "camp," meaning I did not go to their institutes for training, and was not sent out by a recognized missions board.

I was not trained by any camp, just by my local church: First Bible Baptist Church in Hilton, NY, an independent church a little over 50 years old now that has trained and sent out over 180 families in full time service for the Lord. Not sending them off to Bible college, but training them in their own institute and local church and sending them out. I count it such an honor and privilege to be trained by such men at FBBC.

The greatest compliment I ever received from a missionary came when he said, "Bobby, you are the only really independent Baptist missionary I know. We have to answer to our boards or the brethren." I told him I just answer to Jesus and to my local church. We must all have some accountability; I do not consider myself a rebel. I am not an island. I am a part of the body of Christ. I am not your enemy. I have enough of those—the world, the flesh, and the devil. It is just interesting that I can have complete peace entering any Baptist church, because I am going to worship King Jesus. But it seems that if someone hears that so-and-so went to a particular church with a particular pastor, the brethren get mad and now rumors fly and there is a schism in the body.

I was once in a pastors' meeting with around 100 independent Baptist preachers to hear one of the "pillars" of a camp speak. I walked in a little late and sat on the back pew. The place was packed. The preacher was bringing it. I was enjoying it and then he said to all of us, "If you are a pastor, you should always look like one. You should even wear a tie when you're mowing the lawn." I laughed out loud, and almost every pastor turned around and glared at me. I did not get any meetings from that bunch. I love wearing a tie and preach in one most of the time. But if I am working on the lawn, my car, hunting, fishing, I will not be wearing a tie. If you want to, go ahead my brother. Just don't put your limitations on me.

Missionaries can hurt other missionaries by misunderstanding, lack of communication, differing terminology, and many other reasons. I have been lied to, stolen from, blackballed, and gossiped about for years. I even had a missionary steal our land and our truck and then lie to my face about it until confronted by many witnesses in front of a chief. If Jesus had a Judas, we will too. So rub some dirt on it and get back in the game!

I remember in those early days in Zambia begging and pleading with God to send missionaries to help as the work was huge and the time seemed to be perfect. David Livingstone wrote in his diary that he saw the day coming when the African will be converted at every sermon. And it was happening. So many were being saved and needed to be trained and discipled.

We had a missionary visit us from the USA and spend time with us and another group that was in the country. When he returned to the States, he told a Baptist missions board that he could never work with me because I was not a Baptist. Of course, my phone was blowing up in the little office we had opened for communication purposes.

I was told to explain my conversion and baptism. I told them I was saved in a revival meeting in Bryan, Texas, trusting Jesus Christ as my Savior—believing that He died on Calvary, was buried, and resurrected the third day according to the scriptures. A few days later, we moved to Corpus Christi and as I read my Bible through from cover to cover, when I got to the New Testament, I noticed that when someone got saved, they got immersed in water to show the death, burial, and resurrection of Jesus Christ. (In those early days of salvation, I did not know the difference between a Baptist, Catholic, Church of Christ, Mormon... I thought they all believed the same thing. But I knew I did believe the Bible.)

In the time following my salvation, we were attending a non-denominational church, and I asked the pastor what he thought about baptism. He said it was an act of obedience and an identification with what Jesus did for us. It was a picture of his death, burial, and resurrection. So, I asked him to baptize me and he did. Years went by, and after searching for truth, God led us to an independent Baptist church. We were so thankful we had found a church that stood on the absolute truth of the word of God. After many weeks of sitting and listening to the preaching and teaching, it was time to join that local church. I told my pastor that I had been saved. I told him of my baptism, where I was baptized, and by what means I was baptized, and the church accepted our statement of faith and we became members of First Bible Baptist Church. We worked in the church for four years, went to their Bible institute, preached, taught, evangelized—anything and everything the church was involved with, we jumped into with both feet. Then God called us as missionaries to the country of Zambia.

But now my conversion was being questioned because I was not baptized in a Baptist church, but a non-denominational one. I had never heard of such a thing. Our support was dropped by churches in the USA one after another because of these rumors about my baptism, and that I was not a Baptist because I was not baptized in a Baptist church.

As it turns out, I was about to have my first introduction to Baptist Brider doctrine. A brider is someone who thinks that only those baptized in a Baptist church are a part of the bride of Christ. Remember, there is a physical body and a spiritual body. One can be a member of a local Baptist church and still be lost. But one who is in the church, the spiritual body of Christ, cannot be lost. Even though I was not baptized in a Baptist assembly, according to the word of God, my faith in Christ had placed me into the worldwide body of Christ.

1 Corinthians 12:13 For by one Spirit are we all baptized into one body, whether we be Jews or Gentiles, whether we be bond or free; and have been all made to drink into one Spirit. 14 For the body is not one member, but many.

We had to come home to raise support. As I was sitting in my pastor's office, the phone rang from a missions board director whose churches had been supporting us faithfully. The director asked my pastor if he would baptize me again. I remember my pastor asking the question, "Doctor So-and-so, are you a brider?" He said no. So my pastor asked him why he was requesting that I get re-baptized if he was not a brider. The director said that many churches which supported their board and missionaries would drop their support if they kept me on without being baptized again. My pastor answered and asked, "So it's a money issue, then?" He then followed up with, "Why would they try and usurp their authority over another local church when FBBC had accepted Bobby's baptism? Whose money do you want? Theirs or ours?" There was silence on the end of the phone for a few seconds, and then the director said, "We accept Bobby's baptism." Wow, my first introduction to the Baptist Brider doctrine.

Many churches called me and asked me what happened when I was confronted, and I never told them, because I did not want to create a schism in the body. Souls were too important.

There are many Baptist Briders out there, and I love them and thank God people are getting saved through their ministries. I remember when I got back to Africa, I was confronted with the missionary who took it upon himself to spread the word about my baptism, and as we talked he reminded me that the only way I could be a member of his local church was that I would have to be baptized again. I told him we did agree on something: I would never be a member of his church. I am content being a member of Jesus's church, the body of Christ. This same missionary even re-baptized several people whom I had baptized because he didn't consider me a Baptist. Boy, I am glad I'm saved and that Jesus is my Savior!

It is amazing the times I have arrived at a church only to be greeted with questions about my sending church or people I have had meetings with. Some pastors would not support anyone who had any fellowship with so-and-so. Sometimes they wouldn't support me because they had heard that our church allowed someone they did not like in their pulpit. I have played on many teams in sports. But I thought believers were all on the same team, fighting against the flesh, devil, and this world. I have been told I am not a Baptist, and I have been told that I am the only true independent Baptist. Make up your mind.

I truly love pastors. They are God's men for God's people. I have met some of the finest shepherds out there. Their love for the people that God had entrusted to them is contagious. Their love for their wives and children and the brethren goes to the maximum degree. I thank the Lord for the countless list of men who have crossed my path to sharpen my way. You know who you are. If I leave someone out, we might have to rub some dirt on it.

Pastors, I am not your enemy. I want to help you. You have invested in countless others. If I can help you in any way, please let me know. We are on the same team. Culture is different, times are changing, but God's word does not change. Let us not be jealous of one another but rather have a desire to get closer to the One we serve, Jesus Christ!

If you have been hurt, rub some dirt on it. If someone close to you has really hurt you, think about Jesus; He trained twelve men and brought them very close to Himself. One had a devil and betrayed Him. In my life, after training over 150 pastors, twelve of them have turned their backs on the truth, even tried to kick me out of Zambia, sue me, tell lies to our Chief, and do almost everything they could to destroy my name.

If Jesus had one Judas, we will surely have one (or twelve) if we are being conformed to His image.

Chapter Nine

Fear God, Not Man

We previously discussed a little concerning truth. I am so thankful our God is truth; Jesus said He is the way, the TRUTH, and the life (John 14:6).

God is also holy. When we realize God's holiness, our initial reaction should be to see ourselves as unholy. There is a massive gulf between God's holiness and man's holiness. Until we understand the holiness of God, we can never know the depths of our sin. We should shake in our boots when we see ourselves comparing ourselves to Him. Are we deeply pained about our sin? If we are not, do we really understand the holiness of God?

Do we rush into God's presence unaware of just who He is? Worship is much more than a song. When we come into His presence, we need to see Him as holy. Often, it seems man's relationship with God is more of a casual one. It is with a buddy, friend, the man upstairs. Do we understand the price that God has paid for our sins? Too often we come into His presence with no repentance, no confession, no cleansing. Remember, it is by His grace we even have life in our bodies. Do we understand His indignation against sin? The price that was paid in full for you and me?

We sing beautiful songs with thoughts of His love and forgiveness. What about the song that is sung over and over again in heaven?

And the four beasts had each of them six wings about him; and they were full of eyes within: and they rest not day and night, saying, Holy, holy, holy, Lord God Almighty, which was, and is, and is to come. (Revelation 4:8)

How many people today claim to know the Lord, but have never fallen down and truly grieved over their sin? Are we overwhelmed with our own sinfulness? Are we consumed by the holiness of God?

True worshippers come before the Lord with a healthy fear. There are two elements for acceptable worship: reverence and fear. Hebrews 12:28-29 says, "Wherefore we receiving a kingdom which cannot be moved, let us have grace, whereby we may serve God acceptably with reverence and godly fear: For our God is a consuming fire." Worship demands a sense of God's holiness and our sinfulness, with a cry for purging.

We have all heard the phrase, "Judgment is coming." It is a fearful thing to fall into the hands of the Living God. To fear God is to obey what He has commanded and proclaimed in His word. As the wisest man in the Bible said, "Let us hear the conclusion of the whole matter: Fear God, and keep his commandments: for this is the whole duty of man" (Ecc 12:13).

Hebrews 11:7 tells us that Noah obeyed because he was moved with fear. The fear of God moves us not just to reverence, but to obedience. It has a positive result. Obedience brings a shower of love and blessings that flow as a result of doing what God has called us to do. The theme of Deuteronomy is all about obedience and love: to prove our love to God by doing what He has called us to do.

On the other hand, the fear of man brings a snare. We become trapped, unable to get out. This old world and its system use this fear to control the masses. We become so entrenched in what the news and government is throwing at us, causing our hearts and minds to fear the outcome, fear the powers that be, and not to fear God. We walk blindly toward answers that only continue to grip us even more with uncertainty. Where or in whom do we place our trust? Is it in the world? Our government? Man? Science?

When we as a people reject truth, we believe and buy into the lie. When we reject the fear of God, we accept the fear of man and become trapped into thinking that mankind has the answers to our problems, instead of trusting in the Almighty God.

This competition has been going on since the beginning of time. It's a battle over our minds and hearts. Whom shall we fear? Stop listening to the enemy. Fear God and keep His commandments. Rub some dirt on it and get back in the game. It matters.

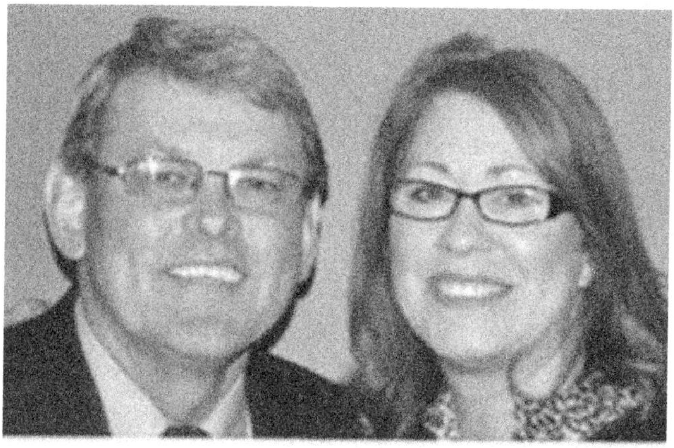

If you enjoyed this resource, you can find many more books and faith-based Bible resources at Living Faith Books

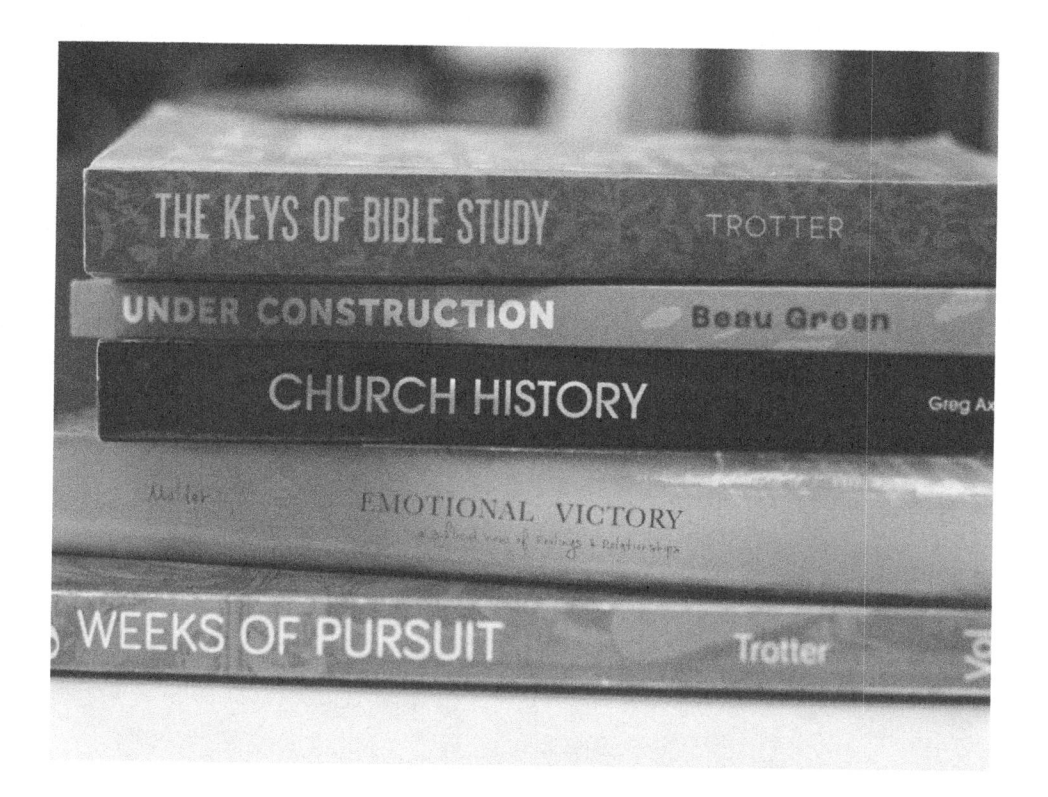

THE KEYS OF BIBLE STUDY — TROTTER
UNDER CONSTRUCTION — Beau Green
CHURCH HISTORY — Greg A
EMOTIONAL VICTORY
WEEKS OF PURSUIT — Trotter

Living Faith Books has published books and biblical materials on many different topics:

- Devotions & commentaries
- Children's ministry
- Ministry leadership
- Church history
- Spiritual developent & formation
- How to study the Bible
- Biblical prophecy
- Evangelism materials
- Marriage & parenting
- Biblical counseling

LIVING FAITH BOOKS

VISIT LFBI.ORG/BOOKS

Made in United States
Orlando, FL
19 October 2023